EXTRa!

ISBN: 978-1-98341-638-5

Illustration and design by Sarah-Leigh Wills.
www.happydesigner.co.uk

EXTRA!

Written by
Kaeleigh MacDonald

Illustrated by
Sarah-Leigh Wills

Every Sunday morning, Lucas goes shopping with Mommy. He likes to sit in the shopping cart and watch the people in the store. Mommy and Lucas were in the baking aisle, to get ingredients for cupcakes, when he noticed a lady whose belly was so big it looked like a round ball under her shirt!

"Mommy," Lucas said. "Why is that lady's belly so big?"
"That lady is going to have a baby," Mommy explained. She smiled at the lady, who patted her big belly and chuckled.

Mommy paused and scratched her head. "Well," she started. "To make a baby, you need . . . a few ingredients. Like when you're baking." She pointed to a cake on the counter. "One ingredient, called sperm, comes from a man. The other, a tiny egg, comes from a woman. Those ingredients mix together in the mommy's belly and that makes a baby. Right there inside! The baby starts off small. Then it grows and grows until it is big enough to be born."

"Do you understand?" she asked.

Lucas thought for a moment. "Yes, I think so."

"You know, not all babies can be made just like that. Sometimes, there needs to be a little extra to make a baby. Like you! You needed extra."

"Extra?" Lucas asked. Mommy nodded "That's right, not all babies are made exactly the same way." Mommy paused and looked at her shopping list. She picked up more sugar and then asked Lucas if he wanted a cookie from the bakery counter.

The cookie was Lucas' favorite part about Sunday shopping. It was even better than riding in the shopping cart. He smiled when the baker handed him a warm chocolate chip cookie and munched it happily as they went to the checkout.

On the way home, Lucas thought about the lady with a baby in her belly and what Mommy had said about him needing extra. It sounded exciting and important, but he didn't really know what it meant. After Mommy and Lucas got home, Lucas went to the park with his friend Eli. They brought Eli's new trucks to play in the sand.

Lucas scooped up sand to make a hill, while Eli drove his digger truck around and around their feet. "Eli?" Lucas asked. "What does extra mean?"
Eli shrugged and looked as confused as Lucas felt.

On the other side of the sandbox, a little girl was playing with cars. She piped up. "Extra is like when you have a little bit of ice cream and someone gives you more."

"Oh!" exclaimed Eli. "Like when I want a second helping of snack?"

"Yes, that's right," said the little girl. "That's extra!"

"Extra must be a very good thing, if it means more," Eli told Lucas. "More is always better!" Lucas agreed that more was always better, and he and Eli took turns adding extra to his mountain of sand. He forgot all about babies while they played.

But later at swimming, he started to think about it again. If he was extra, and extra meant more . . . what was he more of? Lucas saw his friend Jamal diving for rings nearby. Jamal was older and Lucas thought he might know.

So, he told Jamal about being extra. "How can I be extra?" Lucas asked, "What do you think I have extra of?"

Jamal pondered for a moment, and then his face lit up. "The only people I know who have extra anything are superheroes. They have extra powers!"
"Me? A superhero?!"

"Do you glow in the dark?" Jamal asked.
Lucas shook his head no.
"Can you stretch yourself out really far?"
Lucas stretched his arms out as wide as he could, but
they didn't go any further than Jamal's. Jamal shrugged.
"Maybe you don't know your superpower yet. But,
if you're extra, you must have extra powers."
Lucas giggled to himself. A superhero? Wow!

That night, Lucas took the sheet off his bed and tied it around his neck like a cape. He looked at himself in the mirror, and he looked like a superhero! Lucas wondered what powers he would discover, now that he knew he was extra.

He ran down the hall excitedly, his sheet fluttering behind him.
He flew in circles around the living room and bounced on the
couch. Mommy rounded the corner and caught him just as he
leaped toward the coffee table.

"What do you think you're doing?" she scolded.
"I'm extra!" shouted Lucas.
"What do you mean you're extra?"
Lucas grinned broadly at her. "Like you said this morning!
Some babies, like me, take extra. If I have extra powers, then
I'm a superhero!"

"Oh, I see." She sat down on the couch, pulling Lucas onto her lap. "That wasn't what I meant when I said you needed extra. Not like a superhero with extra powers. Instead, it's more like extra ingredients or steps in baking.

For some parents, having a baby isn't as easy as mixing a sperm and an egg together in the mommy's belly. But they want to be a family very badly, and so they find a way. Those babies take a little extra . . ."

"Some kids, like Emmanuel in your class, have two mommies, or two daddies. Remember how you need both sperm from a man and an egg from a woman to make a baby? Those mommies and daddies need to find another person to give them the ingredient they need. Emmanuel's mommies had to get sperm from a special man to help make the baby they wanted.

"Some mommies and daddies aren't able to make a baby inside the mommy's belly. When that happens, their hope for a baby grows first in their hearts. Then, the baby needs to grow in another woman's belly until they are born and can join their family. Like Su-Chin next door."

"Those are some of the ways that a baby might need extra."

Lucas thought for a moment, "Does it take a long time, when a baby needs extra?"

"Yes," she replied. "It can take an extra-long time for parents to welcome home their baby. Those mommies and daddies need to be extra-patient. But, in the end, it's worth it. Without a little extra, we wouldn't have you!" She smiled and kissed the top of Lucas' head.

Lucas looked up at Mommy.

"It took you extra time and extra patience to make me?" She smiled. "Yes, baby, it did."

His eyes lit up with excitement.

"Mommy," Lucas exclaimed, "that means you're extra too!"

Kaeleigh MacDonald

is an infertility author and advocate. She runs the popular infertility blog Unpregnant Chicken, where she writes her musings on the wild world that is 'trying to conceive'. Her son was conceived through in vitro fertilization (IVF) and it was her love of his science-based conception story that prompted this book. She lives in Alberta, Canada with her family.

Made in the USA
Middletown, DE
18 January 2018